Giraffes: 51 Fascinating Facts For Kids

Deborah Sykes

This book is just one of a series of "Fascinating Facts For Kids" books. For more fascinating facts about people, history, animals, and more please visit:

www.fascinatingfactsforkids.com

Contents

Introduction

The giraffe is the world's tallest animal and also one of the most unusual with its long legs and neck.

Giraffes are only found in Africa, although millions of years ago they were found on other continents too.

We hope the following facts will fascinate you and encourage you to find out more about these remarkable animals.

Evolution & History

1. Although the giraffe is only found in the wild in Africa these days, many millions of years ago its ancestors lived in many parts of Europe and Asia.

2. The giraffe's ancestors first appeared in central Asia about fifteen million years ago. However, the earliest fossil records of the giraffe itself, from Israel and Africa, date back about 1.5 million years.

3. Cavemen first came across giraffes about 5,000 years ago and were so impressed that they painted pictures of them in their caves. Some of these paintings were more than twenty-five feet high.

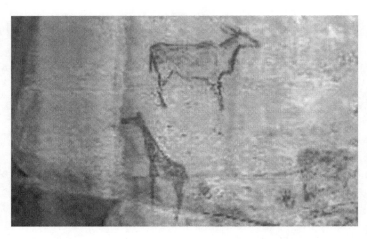

Giraffe rock painting at the Tsodilo Hills, Botswana

4. Early giraffes had short necks which became longer as time went on. There are many theories about why the giraffe developed a long neck - such as for reaching up to the leaves at the top of trees - but nobody knows for sure.

5. For a long time giraffes were called "camel-leopards," because they appeared to be a combination of a camel and a leopard.

Camel   *Leopard*

6. Giraffes were seen again in Europe in the thirteenth century when the Sultan of Egypt presented one to the King of Naples. They were to become the prized possessions of many other rulers across Europe and Asia.

7. Giraffes were first brought to the United States in the early nineteenth century and they soon became the star attractions of traveling circuses.

Anatomy

8. Giraffes are the tallest animals in the world. Adult males can grow to around eighteen feet (5.5 m) and adult females can reach fifteen feet (4.5 m).

The tallest animal

9. Adult male giraffes weigh between 2,400 and 3,000 pounds (1,090 - 1,360 kg), while females weigh between 1,600 and 2,600 pounds (725 - 1,180 kg). The giraffe is one of the world's heaviest land animals.

10. The giraffe has the longest tail of any mammal on earth. It can grow to a length of nine feet (2.75 m).

11. Giraffes' tongues are around eighteen inches (45 cm) long. They are colored blue, as this is thought to protect them from the hot African sun when feeding.

A Giraffe extends its tongue to feed

12. A giraffe's heart is the size of a basketball and the biggest of any land mammal, weighing around twenty-five pounds (11 kg). It pumps 125 pints (60 l) of blood around the body every minute.

13. A giraffe's front legs are longer than its back legs, which means that it has a steeply sloping back.

A giraffe's sloping back

14. The shoulders of a giraffe need to be very strong so that it can hold up its heavy neck and head. The neck and shoulders are joined together with lots of muscles, which means that there is not too much strain on the shoulders from the weight of the neck.

15. The pattern and coloring of a giraffe's coat provide excellent camouflage, meaning they are difficult to spot when standing or roaming among tall trees. Like a human being's fingerprints, each giraffe has a unique pattern on its coat.

The pattern on a giraffe's coat

16. A giraffe has valves in its neck to stop the blood flowing down into the brain when it lowers its head to drink water.

17. The muscles of the nose are strong enough for a giraffe to completely close its nostrils to keep out dust, ants, and sand from sandstorms.

18. Even though it has a long neck, a giraffe has the same number of vertebrae as a human being, although each one can be ten inches (25 cm) long!

19. A fully grown male giraffe has hooves which are the size of dinner plates, about twelve inches (30 cm) across.

20. Both male and female giraffes have a pair of hair-covered horns on their heads called "ossicones." What they are for is not known, as females do not use them for anything, and males only use them when fighting with each other.

A giraffe's ossicones

Habitat

21. Giraffes live on the savannas of Africa. A savanna is a big grassy area of land with trees that are spaced out enough so that sunlight can reach the ground.

22. Giraffes live in eastern, southern, and central Africa. They used to be found in other parts of Africa too, but disappeared from these areas due to hunting.

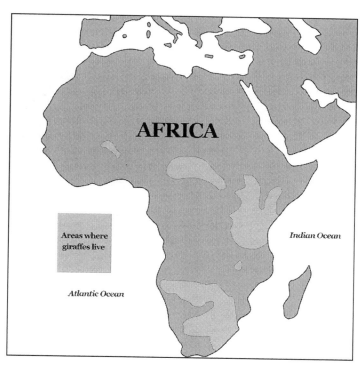

Senses

23. A giraffe uses its eyes, ears, and nose to look out for danger, to find food, and to watch over its youngsters.

24. A giraffe's eyes are located on either side of its head, which gives good all-around vision. Giraffes have excellent eyesight and because they are so tall, they can see for great distances.

25. Giraffes have excellent hearing and a very good sense of smell. They can move their ears to point them at where a sound is coming from.

Feeding & Drinking

26. Giraffes are plant eaters and feed on leaves and buds from trees. Leaves from the acacia tree form the biggest part of a giraffe's diet. They also eat fruit, seeds, and flowers.

A giraffe feeds on an acacia tree

27.   A giraffe's long neck and legs mean it can eat leaves high up in the trees. Male giraffes eat the very highest leaves while females eat the leaves that are closer to the ground.

28.   A giraffe's stomach is divided into four separate chambers that digest food very well. But before food reaches the stomach the giraffe will chew it, bring it back up, and chew it all over again.

29.   Acacia trees have long thorns to stop animals eating their leaves, but these don't stop giraffes! Their thick lips, tongue, and lots of saliva protect them from the sharp thorns.

30.   When drinking at a water hole or river a giraffe must move its front feet apart, bend its knees, and lower its head. This is awkward and dangerous, as lions or crocodiles can easily grab a giraffe when it is bent over.

A giraffe drinks at a water hole

31. Giraffes can go for days without drinking as most of their water comes from the leaves they eat.

Behavior

32. Giraffes travel about in herds, which can be just half a dozen animals or many dozens. Male giraffes - or "bulls" - mainly live in herds with other bull giraffes, while female giraffes - or ""cows" - prefer to be part of a female-only herd. Older bulls often live alone.

A herd of giraffes

33. Young bulls try to establish their dominance in a herd by "necking" with each other. Two bull giraffes will wrap their necks around each other, and swing them to head-butt the other animal's body.

34. Necking is not usually dangerous. The fights are often over in a few minutes with the loser just walking away.

Two giraffes necking

35. Giraffes spend most of their time feeding, with most of the rest spent looking for food or digesting what they have just eaten.

36. Giraffes need very little sleep, sometimes as little as twenty minutes a day. They often sleep standing up during the day and normally lie down only at night.

Baby Giraffes

37. A newborn giraffe, or "calf," weighs about 220 pounds (100 kg) and is over six feet (1.8 m) tall - taller than many human adults!

38. A newly born calf will be standing up within twenty minutes of its birth and walking after an hour.

A giraffe and its calf

39. During its first week, a calf will grow over one inch (2.5 cm) each day, and after one year will have doubled its height.

40. Female calves are fully grown by the age of five and male calves by the age of seven.

41. A young bull is ready to leave its mother at the age of around fifteen months, when it will join other young males to form a herd. Young cows leave their mothers at around eighteen months, but will usually stay in the same area as their mothers.

42. A female giraffe may have six or seven baby giraffes during her lifetime.

Movement

43. Unlike most other four-legged mammals, a giraffe walks by moving both legs on one side of its body forward at the same time, followed by both legs on the other side.

A giraffe walking

44. When it is running, a giraffe moves both back legs forward at the same time, followed by both front legs. The long neck and heavy head also move backward and forward to help with balance.

45. The long, strong legs of a giraffe means it can run at speeds of up to thirty-seven miles per hour (60 kph) over short distances, and ten miles per hour (16 kph) over longer distances.

Assorted Giraffe Facts

46. The giraffe has a relative, the okapi, which lives in the Central African country of Congo. The okapi is a similar shape to the giraffe, but has a much shorter neck.

An okapi

47. Although a calf's mother can give powerful kicks to get rid of any predator, around half of all giraffe calves do not survive their first year.

48. The scientific name for a giraffe is "giraffa camelopardalis" which means "one who walks quickly; a camel marked like a leopard."

49. Large animals usually have slow heartbeats, but a giraffe's heart beats around 150 times every minute - more than twice every second!

50. A healthy giraffe will live to the age of around twenty-five years in the wild, and about twenty-eight years in captivity.

51. The first few months of a giraffe's life are the most dangerous, as this is when it is most at risk of attack by lions, hyenas and leopards.

For more in the Fascinating Facts For Kids series, please visit:

www.fascinatingfactsforkids.com

Illustration Attributions

Giraffe rock painting at the Tsodilo Hills, Botswana
cj Huo, CC BY-SA 1.0
<https://creativecommons.org/licenses/by-sa/1.0>, via
Wikimedia Commons

Camel
Jjron
https://creativecommons.org/licenses/by-sa/3.0/deed.en
https://creativecommons.org/licenses/by-sa/3.0/legalcode

The tallest animal
Bernard DUPONT from FRANCE, CC BY-SA 2.0
<https://creativecommons.org/licenses/by-sa/2.0>, via
Wikimedia Commons

A giraffe's ossicones
D. Gordon E. Robertson, CC BY-SA 3.0
<https://creativecommons.org/licenses/by-sa/3.0>, via
Wikimedia Commons

A giraffe feeds on an acacia tree
Steve Garvie from Dunfermline, Fife, Scotland, CC BY-SA 2.0
<https://creativecommons.org/licenses/by-sa/2.0>, via
Wikimedia Commons

Two giraffes necking
hyper7pro, CC BY 2.0
<https://creativecommons.org/licenses/by/
2.0>, via Wikimedia Commons

A giraffe walking
(WT-en) Jpatokal at English Wikivoyage, CC BY-SA 3.0
<https://creativecommons.org/licenses/by-sa/3.0CC BY-SA 3.0
Creative Commons Attribution-Share Alike 3.0>, via Wikimedia
Commons

An okapi
Charles Miller, CC BY 2.0
<https://creativecommons.org/licenses/by/
2.0>, via Wikimedia Commons

Made in United States
Troutdale, OR
11/27/2023

14959867R00015